This book belongs to:

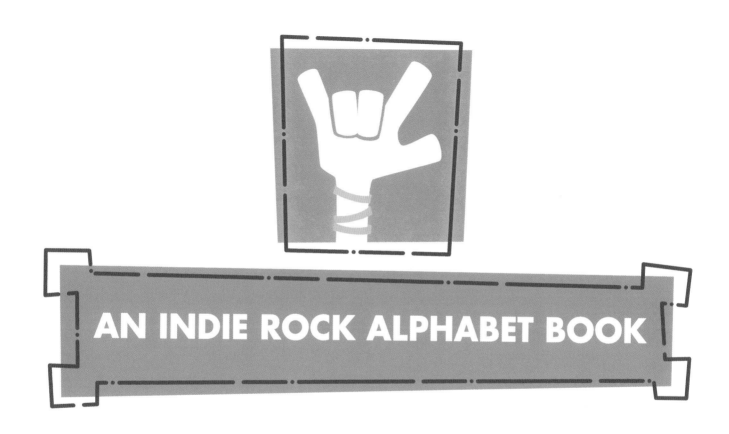

# AN INDIE ROCK ALPHABET BOOK

written by **Caren Kelleher, Kate Kiefer** and **Rachael Maddux**
illustrated by **owen the owen.**
presented by Paste

For Lily and Liam.

**ANIMAL COLLECTIVE** is one weird band, but weird tastes good with *Strawberry Jam.*

Musical snobs and scholars agree:
**BELLE AND SEBASTIAN** are perfectly twee.

That lady from Atlanta is as pretty as a flower.

Her mom named her Chan but she goes by **CAT POWER.**

**DEERHUNTER**'s noisy and the kids think it rocks.
Boys wear dresses too, just ask Bradford Cox!

**ELLIOTT SMITH** is the king of lo-fi.

His story and his music make a lot of people cry.

Some think it's pretty and others think it's odd.
**THE FIERY FURNACES** are a brother-sister squad!

Though **GILLIAN WELCH** was raised in L.A.,
her songs are rooted in the Appalachian clay.

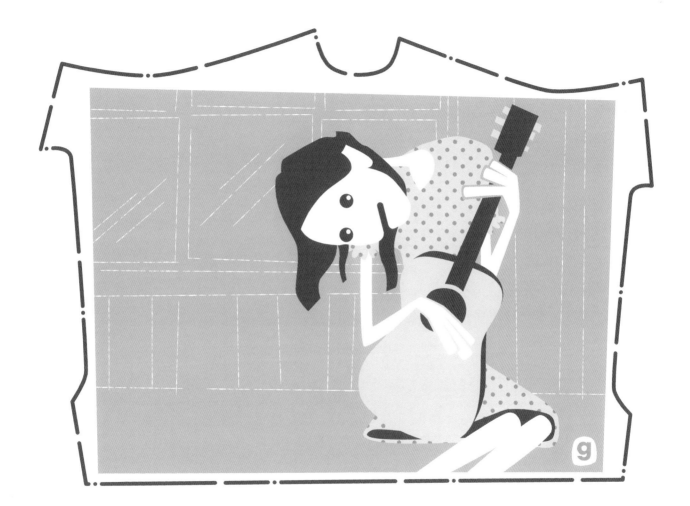

Loud before quiet and beer before juice.
Beans are like peas; **THE HOLD STEADY**'s like Bruce.

**IRON & WINE** is a man named Sam Beam.

He'll make you feel better when you have a bad dream.

Addition or subtraction, it's an easy decision.
I'd rather get down to **JOY DIVISION!**

**KINGS OF LEON** want to dance,

but can't 'cause of their too-tight pants.

Always tell the truth. You must understand
that the only good **LIARS** are an art-rock band.

It used to be a secret but the world caught on.
**MODEST MOUSE** made waves with a song called "Float On."

Four-star inns and resorts are swell,
but they can't compare to **NEUTRAL MILK HOTEL.**

Don't talk to strangers. Never, ever whine,
and learn to play piano like **OVER THE RHINE.**

Stone Temple Pilots turned into tools,
but after all this time, **PEARL JAM** still rules.

**?UESTLOVE** and Black Thought are in cahoots on their jazzy hip-hop band, The Roots.

Birthdays, puppy dogs, breakfast in bed...
Nothing could be better than **RADIOHEAD.**

No matter which religion you choose,
always believe in the **SILVER JEWS.**

I'd listen all day if I had the choice
to Mr. **TOM WAITS** and his growly voice.

Though **UNCLE TUPELO** met an early demise,

from the ashes did Son Volt and Wilco arise.

**VAMPIRE WEEKEND** is hot, or so we're told.

But will they be around when you're another year old?

**WEEZER** used to rock—it's crazy, but it's true!
Two words for you, kid: *Pinkerton* and blue.

John Doe's name is boring, but his music is not.
When it comes to punk, his band **X** marks the spot.

Truer words have never been spoken:
**YO LA TENGO**'s the best band from Hoboken.

**THE ZOMBIES** may sound like four guys from Liverpool, but *Odessey and Oracle* is still pretty cool.

Now I know my indie scene!
Next time won't you rock with me?

THE
END

*Paste* is an entertainment magazine.
We write about signs of life in music, film and culture.
www.pastemagazine.com

Kate Kiefer and Rachael Maddux are editors at Paste.
Caren Kelleher used to be Paste's marketing director,
but now she goes to graduate school at Harvard.

owen the owen possesses the ability to fold things
that are not normally thought of as things one would fold,
and spends massive sections of his time burrowing,
deep beneath the Earth's crust, in search of snacks.

Made in the USA